T0114991

THE GOLDEN KEYS—

To Healing the
Spiritual, Emotional, Mental, Physical

LIONEL SABOURIN

BALBOA.
PRESS
A DIVISION OF HAY HOUSE

Author Credits: A well informed teacher and student of life

Balboa Press books may be ordered through booksellers or by contacting:

Balboa Press
A Division of Hay House
1663 Liberty Drive
Bloomington, IN 47403
www.balboapress.com
1 (877) 407-4847

Printed in the United States of America.

ISBN: 978-1-4525-8638-0 (sc)
ISBN: 978-1-4525-8639-7 (hc)
ISBN: 978-1-4525-8706-6 (e)

Library of Congress Control Number: 2013920555

Balboa Press rev. date: 12/19/2013

You are pure Gold,
-- You just don't know or remember

Contents

1

On Our Journey

The most neglected facet of one's being is our intuitive mind or soul mind. It's the greatest resource we have within us. Each of us carries that Diamond Core God Cell, within our heart center. As its ignited to play a part in our lives all the facets of the Creator within are amplified and then it can be further and further uncovered, until it can become so obvious to you. You remember the <u>joy</u> and the Grandeur of you, that you are.

There's a Golden spark inside of you. It's not something that when it comes to a certain point that it goes out, like a candle. It's continuous in this life and every other life and lives that you had and will live. It's the real you, authentic you, it just got covered over and you were made to focus outside of you and then you forgot.

I remember as a little boy, playing outside on the farm. That I was special, or felt special. I was in bliss most of the time that I remember. I had found an old iron wheel about 18" diameter with a shaft through the center of about 4" long each side, by ¾" thick and I used to roll this around the yard, just being. I was always (well most of the time) happy. I can remember being very creative and helpful. I would fill up the wood box piece by piece until it was full, so my mother and sisters had lots of wood for the stove, for heat and to prepare meals etc… Then I would fall asleep by the stove all tired out, but really satisfied with myself that I had done a good job, which made me feel important.

As I grew up things were OK until about 5 years old, then things started to not go as good. I felt less important and small compared to others, self-image and worthiness suffered. My three brothers and eight sisters didn't help either. I was born in 1941 during the war of 39' to 45' and remember becoming conscious of my physical self in 1947.

Becoming conscious of time, space, distance that was quite an experience. Becoming aware of the 3rd. dimension that I was in, before it was just now, always just now. After this is when things started to change as feeling less than; less than just being. I was/felt quite free when I was young, not too many demands were put on me. But then around eight / nine / ten years old, I had to start doing more chores. Making sure the wood boxes were full and coal pails full for the stove and furnace, empty the ashes daily so they would always be empty and clean for morning. Then around 14, my sisters discovered that I could milk cows and was good at it. So that became another chore to do eight to ten cows in the morning and night. Later we got milking machines, which helped, totally about 30 cows.

I never did very well in school at first. The nuns were very biased; they paid more attention to the people who had more money than those that didn't. Maybe because they could donate money and time to help the community more. I didn't like the games people played then, and I still don't, "Competition." I am better than you are; it was always to be better than. What a stink or hypocrite, at least that was my perception then, never did like the game and still don't. What I mean by the game is "the Altered Ego". The alter ego was always to be more / better. I am better then you and one of the ways to be better then you is sometimes to tear the other person down, make the other person lesser. The biggest problem in the world right now is power and control.

I guess that's the way things were. Things are maybe a bit the same now, but I'm sure glad they're changing.

As a youngster I always felt better with the feminine energy. Didn't know what it was then, but the female, I always felt better with. I didn't seem to have to prove myself. It was male energy, male had to prove itself. Forceful /stronger over others. So the old thing was/is then you have to be on top. The best, more than others. As a youngster, I also didn't have the size, mass, that's probably why I developed my intelligence more. Being quick witted and by observation I learnt a lot.

I was also quite intuitive, although I didn't know what that was then, the answers were there for me. Yet this is when I consciously shut down or closed the door to my Greater Self. Because somehow everything in the world seemed to point to, you can't be all that you are. I became a victim of social consciousness. As one becomes more of a victim, one feels less and less important and if you don't feel important then nobody else does either.

Typically everyone is conditioned into and hypnotized into believing a system which is all interjected from outside sources such as parents, teachers, churches, governments, businesses and society. These hypnotic suggestions and overlays upon overlays are unconsciously accepted as truths into a person's belief structure and soon manifest in their everyday life as a reality.

A self-inflicted trap and most of us do it. Decisions are made about ourselves, society, and the world. I will explain the power of decision in another chapter! (chapter 5).

A turning point in life, a catalysis cause by someone saying something or doing something that affects you, losing a Job, an accident, the ending of a relationship. This is a point usually where a person makes a decision about the self or something else about reality that alters ones path.

The solution of today becomes the problem of tomorrow, because it is based on a partial picture, lower truths, not higher deeper truths and not the big picture.

CHAPTER

2

Improving of Self-Image

This started in 1968. It was suggested by my boss, owner of the company doing kitchen cabinets, that I should register to take a Dale Carnegie course, on public speaking and dealing with the public. Because he had put me in charge of a certain part of the company. I was dealing with new home owners and contractors so this would than help me in dealing/working with them. Of course, this would help the company. His motto was always "profit/money," which was interpreted as power.

He is still the same today 45 years later. Although his heart was in the right place, it didn't always turn out that way.

This was a 10 week course, costing $275.00 then. That was a lot of money for me in those days. Every week we were to give a short talk 60/90 seconds on a particular subject. Open /Deliver / Close.

On the 4th. or 5th. week I didn't think I was doing very well. Poor self-image. View of self was not seen as valuable. I was going to quit but then something happened on the 6th week. Because we could pick our own subject. For some reason or another, I chose a subject I knew well and I was passionate about. So in doing so, I came from the heart, a knowingness, a feeling not from the mind. And for some reason made a big hit with my talk. At the break people were asking me a lot more questions. Complimenting me on my delivery and talk and that made me feel very good about myself. I sort of knew way down deep there was something, but on the surface and what I had been told about myself was not very good.

In the old school, the old world of polarity, you're nobody until we say you're somebody. It's always they, they got the power…they… and if you don't go by what they say, by they I mean the system "mass consciousness", then they can always take it away from you. It's a system that self equalizes itself. So that nobody can get too big??? It's also a tear down system. They pull you down so they can get up, and become more. It's a system built on duality/polarity, competition. And it works well to a point, then it seems to or can have a reverse effect, depending on the view of one self.

Competition is used as a motivation to be and to have, but there are always two sides to it: win and/or lose. It's a self-regulating system it's set up in a negative energy to divide and conquer, humanity does that!!!!! It's an energy that produces war etc…

<u>Teens</u>

Then as a teen, other things started to kick in. Hormones. Energy and they usually start at the bottom- the base. These are chakras, energy centers in the body. But of course, not knowing any of these things (chakras) at the time, you're a physical being and one usually gives in to them. One's spirit does not fully enter in the body until ten to twelve years old. This is when the full life force, the chi, sexual energy, prana enters into the body.

This is a time of lots of struggle within self. One wants to follow the natural flow of things, the energy- urges, and desires. In then clicks in your belief structure of society and of course, your self-image. And if you have a poor view of self, guess what, you're not going to attract the best. You're not worthy of and then settle for the left over's and crumbs. Then you attract and are attracted to like-minded people. The old saying- the rich get rich because of... and the poor are poor because of... It's always a self inflicting prophecy, and of course being brought up like that one usually lives life like that.

Our beliefs about ourselves and values create our world, like attracts like. In growing up, we don't know of this nor are we taught anything like it. School was reading, writing, and arithmetic. And you're taught through repetition. Repeat. Repeat. Home-work. Home-work. Hoping that things will sink in, you lose your own individuality, and put into a mold.

I learnt this later, but did you know that the system is <u>designed</u> for you to fail? Yes fail! And if you make it through then they call them <u>leaders.</u> Wow, you made it through you must be good. You must be a leader then, <u>know</u> wonder most of us grow up twisted, bent all out of shape, and become mostly dysfunctional and we become like sheep. The pack/followers of a system, mass consciousness. Then when you try to break free from the system they call you an outcast, you don't fit in. That's why so many people can't function.

Things in the system started to change big time in the fifties, more in the sixties. But the fifties were called the hippie movement, long hair and such; they gave up on the system, and wanted to learn <u>outside</u> of the box. They found the box too restrictive.

One does not want to restrict spirit, so their own spirit was trying to be free. Free from bondage, being molded, and to start reshaping the system.

I grew up in a family and system where the value of self is not important. Your part of the family of the system. Don't think/feel that your something special. You're not. If you do, we'll put you in your place. I was born in a family of twelve, being the eight one. You first become part of a system where individuality does not matter.

What I Learnt about Decisions and How They work and Don't work

I followed the system just like everyone else. Started a job in the big city- two months. Then started in a department of transport surveying for road building. I worked my way up the chain, became in charge of a crew etc. Then in 1965, I decided to take my first holiday break ever even though one couldn't afford such, one did.

Just before my return to work in 1965, D.O.T. (Department of Highways) I met with my older brother and he asked if I would like to do cabinets. Well I didn't know squat about carpentry, so I declined and went back to my old job. After a week or so, I kept thinking, "there's no future here. Maybe, just maybe, carpentry." So I phoned and he said, "sure, come on down." That was the catalysis that shifted my path.

What I have learned since and to share with everyone is to go back in your life, reflect back on your life and recall all the points, that catalysis, that affected your path. This is one of the ways the soul, your soul- finds its way. It's a set up, and yet it isn't. This is called reflections -- reflect back into your life and you'll find, recognize the triggers that cause you to make shift in your life.

I started in home finishing and cabinetry. Kept learning and learning, but about six months later, I was frustrated and had intentions of going back to D.O.T. (Department of Transportation). That night my brother and I had a talk about money and such, etc. Well I went home, upset and angry about everything, yet, yet somehow, that was again the catalyst that got me to make a decision. A decision about, I'm going to learn this cabinet business even if it kills me. That's what turned everything around. That push, that energy, was what motivated me forward to master cabinet making. And I did. I became a master cabinet maker. And I still am, and enjoying it. But now, I'm also an instructor in self-development, self-empowering, self-awareness.

CHAPTER

3

Struggling

I'm at the place of where I made a decision to learn cabinet making. Still am and enjoying it. But now, I'm an instructor of Self Development and Self Awareness and Self Realization. So now more on the next catalysis that triggered the next move!!!

As in mastering cabinetry, and being in charge of managing multiple crews in the work force and dealing with more contractors and home owners. My boss suggested that I take Public

Relations Training. And so, I registered for a Public Speaking (Dale Carnegie) training of which I wondered "why had I done such a thing."

See, I had been struggling with an internal self-worth issue. So in that ten week course finally about the 6th week in the course, I did a talk for the crowd of which I got recognition for. That made a big difference in myself realization, why because my talk had come from something I knew. I was confident. I knew what I was saying (talking about). That was another turning point (catalyst) of getting me to go in a certain direction.

So I kept on taking training that I thought would lead to success. I guess the point or goal for people is always to push for success. There's always a drive to do better/more. So I kept taking other training that I thought were supposed to lead to success.

I was always fascinated with the mind. If you think a certain way, it's supposed to lead to success. If you think another certain way, it leads to failure. So there was no right way of thinking or wrong way of thinking. It's just that thinking in a certain way, gave you one of those results.

So then I took one more training course and this one seemed to put all the others together one tool box instead of ten.

I discovered latent talents and abilities that each and every one of us has to varying degrees.

Clairsentience, Clairvoyance,
Clairaudience, Cognition
And even telepathy.

To learn the art of meditating and experiential imagery, (that's beyond meditation) dimensional perception to other worlds, etc. A whole new world had opened up, Healing and distance healing, wisdom and knowingness. This was all very good because it just kept opening up <u>new</u> doors and awareness.

But I want to interject here. A very important point:

> Information= This is all leading
> up to something. Something that
> was only discovered later on.

So by following through with this story you'll find what the discoveries will be. Actually it was all about the self. To get to know the self. Self-Realization, Self-Awareness, Etc. And self is ever evolving.

HA! But then to what???

See, were not told really anything when we're growing up because no one really knows. Everyone is caught up in duality/polarity and trying to make/earn a living, and live life.

And everyone else is trying to sell everyone else. What they think and maybe discovered what the key is.

In 1977 -- I met a man "Mickael Blake Read" that tapped into universal Mind, Mikael did the same kind of work as Edger Casey did known as the "sleeping Prophet" back in the early 20's & 30's &

40's. Casey died in 1945 and his work is still being studied in Virginia Beach, United States.

Mickael seemed like an ordinary man, did editing for the Toronto paper, flew his glider plane and was instructing others how to fly. When I met him in 1977 he was wanting to break the record of how long one could stay in the air with these planes. He was curious about the wind draft coming out from the Canadian Rockies, that would keep him afloat for a longer period of time.

My good friend Mikael past over to the other side in late January 2013, he will be missed by many.

My first interaction with Mickael and the Group of Entities, numbering between six and a half thousand (6500) to seven thousand (7,000) as a collective group spoke through Mikael.

As Mickael would put himself in a relaxed hypnotic state he would then connect to these entities, called "The Evergreens" that was a name given to them by his wife "Phillippa". Once the connection was made Phillippa would then start asking questions to the Evergreens, and Mickael fast asleep would answer.

As I'm watching this take place I'm in Awe, how does this work? I had the privilege of interacting with these beings, called the Evergreens, and they just blew my mind. I had never heard such wisdom in my life, and it made sense.

My curiosity got the best of me, so I decided to book a private session with these beings from another dimension, the UNSEEN.

That decision and choice to interact with these other beings from other dimensions, put me on a fast track of my Spiritual development. Unknown to my personal physical self, my spirit self, my High Self, established a contract, an agreement, to continue to interact with these beings for at least another 18 years or so.

Two to three times a year I would book a time with Michael so that I could interact with these beings called the Evergreens.

What they would reveal to me was always enlightening, answers to my questions that were beyond my wildest expectations and then some. Instead of highering a business consultant, a financial consultant, I would book with the Evergreens. The time and money that they saved me, I don't think I can ever put a price on.

At this point I'd like to leave a copy of what the Evergreens gave us as a living philosophy to live life by, and it's called the 8 phrases.

A living Philosophy by,
"The Evergreens"

1. I am the result of me.
2. I'am more, I'am never less.
3. I discover newness about me each and every day.
4. I act because in action is decay.

5. I speak because the words need to be said.
6. I'am the right person.
7. I have no enemies, only friends I have yet to meet.
8. I have no masters but myself.

I've always enjoyed these, because it helped me take responsibility for my actions and choices, instead of blaming others. If one blames others, or the world it's like giving your power away to an external force, leaves you powerless.

By taking responsibility for everything that I do, everything I create, allows me to feel more powerful and in command of my life. I create my reality.

So if there is a mistake or error, one can learn from this, what's the gift?

That is a really, really good question to ask oneself, "What is the gift in this"? If you give it enough time you'll find it.

But back to the basics of my path...

In learning about meditation, visualization, focus, and just learning about healing. Healing the body - the mental/emotional/spiritual was/ is very good- but, but, but. In all of that there was a problem- some things worked, and some things didn't. Why?

In not knowing, one keeps on trying. It's like shooting in the dark. And one of the big problems sometimes is because one does not really know what one is looking for. Most people don't really know what they want when asked!!! Yet lots know of what they don't want, which is what they mostly get, because that is the focus.

Gradually I learned to go where I'm pulled, it's like a magnet.

There's a magnet (energy) and one is a magnet (energy) and by allowing and following the pull, usually it's the right place/thing/experience that answers a few questions. Which then can lead to other questions.

I've since learned that we all have, what is called a "MAGNETIC MONOPLE" in our strum, just above the solar plexus in the body. This is a magnet that has only one poll, it attracts things to you or you to it. This is what spirit uses to move you somewhere, so go where you're being pulled. This is also the law of attraction at its finest.

4

Another new chapter in my life

Right now I'm in Hawaii sitting by a big Banyan tree writing this. Reflecting on the past that has led me here, hoping that I can help, develop, and bring "Signature Cell Healing" a modality to Canada that was developed by "Kahu Fred Sterling" of Hawaii.

Now before I go any further here, we will back up one step to say, another big piece of the puzzle is that Elly Roselle, in 1984 discovered a process of going with in the subconscious and called it "Core Belief Engineering" and that was a process that allowed an individual to go back into one's past and to review or have the ability to review with a 'facilitator' that knows how to guide one back into the past and review from another perspective. The ability to see what one chose – and the decision that was chosen then of that reality at that time.

That decision made then, no longer applies to today, it's out dated.

That one time solution has now become the problem. That decision made then, no longer applies today, it's out dated. Know when you buy food from a store: "it's good until such and such a date", well everything now in your memory (subconscious mind) is dated, So if it's out dated and has **_no more value_** would you exchange it for something better? Why keep listening to a voice that has no more value? Would you be ready to exchange it?

What would you truly give in exchange for what you truly want?

One big/main reason- the subconscious/ unconscious- does not/may not know that time has gone by and is still in the past and /or still trying to protect self from harm etc... We call that now today as comparison to computer that there's a virus in the program. Or there's a bug in the hard drive it may have picked up a bug. So then one has to de-bug the hard-drive/remove the virus <u>from the software etc.</u>

Many words could be used to describe this. So in this I will call it aspects/parts of the self. We have -- one has developed many aspects/parts of the self. Say every decision one made, every choice that was made- is creating another aspect. So now everyone has many 1,000's of aspects (parts) within.

Now as these aspects (parts) are within, there within the subconscious, unconscious, and are operating as if no time and without judgment.

The aspects (parts) are only doing within the self what the self has chosen as a truth, as a reality.

Then it continues to do that task devotedly.

Choice – Options – Alternatives

Where & when did you decide to be poor?
Where & when did you decide to be sick?
Or have poor health?
Where & when did you decide about relationships?
Where & when did you decide, choose to limit your Abundance?
So does one know everything that one chose/ decided on many years ago? Not usually.

Most people are doing quite well on their path, but those that aren't- it's best to look back, review, and re-decide again from a different perspective. And with the help of a facilitator, it's much easier. Look and review all past aspects one created and see if one still agrees in the present moment of those decisions and choices one did in the past. Let's look at it this way – I'm a result of me, and

I have no masters but myself. Cause and Effect and back to Cause, we are our own Self-fulfilling Prophecy.

Now back to my path

Upon discovering core belief engineering (a really good tool), I've been calling it "REVERSE ENGINEERING", go back in and re-view the original decision, the original CAUSE and re-decide again. One can and does modify & continue to modify the self, ever growing, ever expanding, only self didn't really know to what. One looked at potentials yet potentials was a loose / open word. Then because of the original person that discovered CBE, was experiencing difficulty in expanding & such, I decided to take sabbatical for a couple of years and that expanded to 7 years.

Then upon seeing the world changing & others changing and in 1998 with new information being revealed from the universe, decided to get back into instructing self-development

& Self Awareness. In the 1990's many more entrepreneurs, and instructors came on board to help bring more light on to the world.

Upon getting back involved in helping people discover their hidden talents & abilities, the world was constantly evolving / changing, new energies were being brought in from the great Central sun through our solar sun to the very core of sentient Mother earth, (known as GAIA). So the tools work. It's a matter of understanding them at a very deep level, even to the very core of self. Even now my own self needs to evolve more & to the next level.

A Magnetic Pull

In 2001 March, the energy was pulling at me so strong to sign up and go to, what was called "the mid-summer life conference" by Lee Carroll & Kryon (Kryon known as the magnetic Master in the universe). I was not accustomed to that kind of pull / draw. But upon registering that one night in March, the next day it had totally relaxed. It was like knowing that, that had been the right thing to do.

Enjoyed that week-end, felt like I had grown / evolved but not knowing to what degree or level. No bench mark to compare to.

Then in 2002 did not go but in 2003 did again go to the mid-summer light conference and it's like I had left the cocoon and became the butter fly. Everything was different, I felt different and that's when everything started to change. I had given permission to my soul to help in the change. I wanted to get more involved in instructing classes ETC… and my wife also then made a decision about her life. I didn't know of it until 3 / 4 months later that she wanted to separate and go for a divorce. --- WOW what's going on here?

Now that was something I did not expect, did not want to experience ---- But Spirit had other things in mind, and it was aware of the overview, of which I was not. Later learnt that in my human design (DNA blueprint) that I have a channel of Innocence. In other words I usually don't make assumptions.

I was told later by spirit from the other side of the veil, that it was a good thing that it had happened, that it was complete. I did not have to repeat / to learn again, so then I could go on to my next spiritual contract. In other words our spirit (soul) loads on many contracts, just in case the lessons are learned and then a person can go on to the next contract in the same life. In this case (my case) I'm able to complete my lessons now in 3rd dimension & go on. I don't have to die & come back in another body to start over again and continue. I can continue in this same body on to the next life experience. By the way that's called Ascension in this new energy in this now time. Now I have a clean clear canvass in front of me to paint / create what I choose.

In a relationship when a person's vibrations starts to climb, to accelerate and the other person hangs on to the past the harmony that was starts to disappear.

There needs to be some kind of harmony when one is in a relationship, but when one wants to stay in the past and create drama, it starts to create a dis-harmony.

What's been learned about those that create drama in their lives is that it helps them feel more alive.

On Beliefs

One thing that I've learn is that the body is a reflection (a mirror) of one's inner beliefs.

For example; -

Rheumatoid arthritis inflammation of the joints. Now there's many types of arthritis and to me arthritis has to do with resistance. A person is resisting change usually fear based and mostly if not always at an unconscious level. A person does not even know what their resisting, there not conscious of what it is. So rheumatoid arthritis is hanging on to deeply held RIDGET beliefs. There not flexible, that's why it affects the joints, any joint and the hands can even puff up considerably.

An-other way of seeing this is the people that can tell the weather is going to change is by the pain in their bodies. The reason for this is that our bodies are a small magnetic field, and the weather is also a magnetic field. Say it can be a low which is damper, and a high which is drier. So say that a low in the weather pattern is coming in off the west coast, a person in land can already feel it, they can feel it in there joints and they can say the weather is going to change. The reason behind this is that the body is a small magnetic and the weather also magnetic but it's perceived as a foreign energy, a threat to the body so it's responding by resisting. Again arthritis.

CHAPTER

5

This has not been done before

First clear the self, learn to love self, clear & bring up to date all aspects of self. Have a good relationship with self, which is the same as relationship to soul. Once a person realizes this, one is self-realized, is self-aware. Then one can complete and not necessarily need to return & experience 3D again. To limit, to restrict, slow things down in order to understand life --- light.

So then one can be in 3D but not of it, move on beyond polarity / duality and be in neutral.

Like a pendulum not to swing to the left or the right, to stay in the middle as much as one can. One may go off center every now and them, but it's best to come back to center, neutral and not get caught up in polarity, people's drama.

Yet I find there is residue left from the past. Old aspects of the past, of self keep coming up in the present in the now to be resolved, brought forward & then integrated into the new you. Not an easy process.

Let me explain my analogy, my "scenario" of aspects, what an aspect is & how they work in us, in our minds. Another word we could use to describe this is parts, parts of our self or aspects of our selves.

Imagine this now, play the game with me here, so as to understand aspects. Imagine there's a big ship, I mean a big ship. It's a ¼ mile long and at-least 150 ft. wide, and has 10 / 11 floors or so. This now is the body and mind together here now. The ship say is the body and everyone on board is parts of you or aspects of you, so it's all you.

Ok imagine this now, at birth (when your born) say the ship is empty because your new, it's new. So at first it's mostly your mother that feeds you and clothes you, otherwise you would not survive. So at first one is very dependent on one's mother, the father to, but for this now let's stay with the mother. Survival depends on others at first, and the mind is like a sponge it observes and takes everything in. It starts to develop path ways in the brain, of this and of that and other things. The tastes the textures, the smells, the images, and on & on & on. Every now and then it *"may"* make an internal decision on & about what it's learning & experiencing.

<u>DECISIONS</u> and the impact on our lives

Now the key word here is "DECISION"

This is what caused the distortion of reality of truth. When we left the other side of the veil to come to 3D we hid ourselves (our God self, our divine self) from our self, we put on a mask, so we could stay in 3D the physical world. In doing so we chose to limit ourselves to our 5D senses (taste, touch, smell, sound, seeing,) & the 6th. sense intuition and the 7th. knowingness we gradually let go of the last two, and start to just concentrate and focus on the 5 physical senses.

Now in the physical world our perceived world, one makes decisions on what's happening. A decision is like ridigitizing / solidifying in time and space from something fluidity. That is what is called illusion, we crystallize an energy that is fluid (not solid) and make it solid, and we construct a truth.

PERCEPTION

Everything is perception, and at first in our very early years the mind is like a sponge. The mind perceives things seen and unseen and will make decisions on different experiences as it goes through its first years. As parents, because of what we learn from our parents, we pass on to them our beliefs, values & truths of what is real and what isn't real. So one is conditioned, brainwashed into thinking what is real and what is not. That's the first step of creating *"Paranoia"* in the child. As were growing up (being child) one does not have full knowledge of how to yet. How things actually work, & one is not in any position of Power. To make changes / to choose differently. So we make decisions about things – we experience things (life) that we really can't complete, so we have a lot of incomplete experiences.

That decision made then, no longer applies today, it's out dated. Know when you buy food from a store: "it's good until such and such a date".

Everything now in your memory (subconscious mind) is dated, So if it's out dated and has _no more value_ would you exchange it for something better? Why keep listening to a voice that has no more value? Would you be ready to exchange it?

<u>What would you truly give in exchange for what you truly want?</u>

Another version or way of putting this is, as we were growing up, typically everyone was conditioned into and hypnotized into believing a system which was all interjected from outside sources, such as parents, teachers, churches, governments, businesses and society. These hypnotic overlays upon overlays were unconsciously accepted as truths into a person's belief structure and soon manifested in their everyday life.

These experiences still have energy and that is one of the reasons of what causes problems in our later years. Incomplete experiences that want to complete, but one does not have an out yet. These are like seeds waiting in the wind (ground, in our unconscious mind) to germinate, that's why things can be dormant for years and then surface later in one's life.

Now as we get older in years, we can feel like being held back and can't seem to figure it out. It can be very frustrating and discouraging. We want to make progress in our lives, our business, our careers and relationships, but it's like some invisible force & resistance just seems to be keeping us from having the life we really want.

Our childhood conditioning has a pervasive & insidious grip on us, controlling our behavior and decision making, keeping us locked into a very limited level of self-expression and enjoyment of our lives. That is because we have made *__"feeling level decisions"__* before we developed verbal language skills. These are usually experienced as conflicting, disruptive energy wave patterns held in the body, which usually cancels out conscious intentions even now as an adult.

That's why affirmations don't really work. These inner conflicts show up as problems with our health, relationships, work, careers, busyness and home.

This is why will power alone or intellectual approaches like affirmations, self-help books, reasoning, conventional counseling, coaching and cognitive therapy just can't get at them. Only the direct experience of resolution and the clearing of incomplete energies out of the system (one's body) can provide the shift required to create true inner and outer permanent change.

True change comes from the restructuring of an Idea, into new possibilities, restore & renew, it's what nature does. Cause to effect back to Cause again, ebb & flow.

CHAPTER

6

Finding the Internal Light (Spark)

Those that know that there's an inner spark within them do not fear the furnace. We come to planet earth with this spark inside of ourselves, but we hide it from ourselves and from others. We do this for our own protection, so we hide it, then it gets covered over with layers and layers of others perception, others substance / contamination cling to it. Gradually it gets covered over & for some becomes distinguished and barely lit, in other words many have given up hope.

Now for some, because of choices & experiences, when you discover this spark again you do not fear the furnace. You don't fear being judged by others, because you know that they don't know this, I learned this after my death experience. (it was a conscious choice to come back).

Some people will put themselves through tests after test, after tests to prove to themselves that there is a Divine Spark within. Love does not need to be tested, it is, always was, al--ways will be, and you'll find that love does not / will not follow the old paradigm / old path. Because it would find a new path, (not the norm) & that's one of the reasons many people don't, because they may not want to appear different, for some it's pretty scary. In the old school to be different was to be a target, the unknown is too scary.

FEARFUL

Many people fear the furnace and yet that's where – when all the impurities are removed your clear again. As with gold what do they do? They put the gold in the furnace to remove all the impurities from within it, so what's left is pure gold.

You are pure gold, always was – al-ways will be that will never change. Yet as we come to planet earth to experience contrast and to experience the experience of experiencing and lots of things will cling on to you as you go through your day. Lots of say impurities will be attracted & attach themselves to you and gradually one forgets or is told by others that you're not pure and if you buy that, then gradually one becomes like them and forgets of being unique. That's when one's spirit is crushed and the fire (spark) is barely lit.

Remember

Now were going through a time of remembering. Do not fear the furnace, do not fear to be different to be unique, to be yourself (whatever that is), because you are divine made from & with God, pure energy. Your authentic self is wanting to be discovered, re discovered. Will you let / allow your soul to show / reveal itself to you. In the not too distant future all the energy, the dense thoughts of what isn't you will be leaving and go anyway.

In the past and for some that still don't know the system was developed (by some) for people to not know this, to hide this, so they could be in power and for many they still reign with this, using fear as a tool. The system was / is so beautifully disguised that way and know body questions it, we all became slaves / victims to the process, the system. The movie the Matrix is what the system is. Many are still afraid to leave the system, to be different, to create their own path. There are many books and stories, of people that took liberty and destiny in to their own hands and made their own way in life. Some were successful and some were not, some were extricated, thrown out from their own country even.

Please read "<u>Ann Rand book's</u>". Fountainhead & Atlas Shrugged. The Atlas Shrug book, I could not put down, about 1200 pages or so, I started on a Friday evening and finished at about midnight Sunday. Most of the books I'd read before were around 250 to 300 hundred pages, but this just captivated me. Symbolically and as a story she was describing exactly what's going on right now in this planetary shift were now experiencing.

Because it does take courage & strength & energy to plow your own trail, but when you do, you'll find after while that many will follow and gradually there's an evolution, an Evolution into a new time frame a new paradigm.

Lionel Sabourin

Aspects

Let's look at aspects within the self and what are aspects.

You are an aspect of your soul. First let's go back a long, long way back in time, before there was time. God wanting to know all of him, said go out there and experience everything there is to experience, turn over every stone and look into every nook and cranny there is and report back and so on and so on.

So God created an aspect of him / herself and then that aspect created an aspect of itself and then that god created an aspect of itself and on and on. So now your soul created you, the personality you, to come to earth and experience on its behalf. In other words you're an aspect of your Higher Self which is an aspect of the soul. these aspects are all created by you and at different times, only you don't remember.

The best is to be in love with all of your aspects, those that you know and those that you don't know. Create an envoirment in the self (a safe space) that feels good, where one likes to spend time there, with self.

Aspects are sub-personalities that develop an identity of themselves, they are you but different and serve / do a different function. Once developed they have their own perceptions of life, values and beliefs etc…

They're there to help you supposedly, yet every now and then because of their function can sabotage your whole life and maybe that's what you told them to do.

I know I had one that about every seven years or so as I became more and more successful, it would start sabotaging me and with a short period of time I would be broke again. When I was broke it would stop and go into hiding again and let me advance for a while. As I would start making more money again and succeeding again it would be triggered and come back out an start sabotaging me again. About every seven years or so this would happen. There's a pattern here only I was too engrossed in making a living earning money that didn't recognize it.

The aspects / viruses built upon values, belief systems was basically that I didn't deserve it and that I could not become a leader (be the president) of my own company and had to be a follower. That was its perception it's belief about self because of a decision that was made at 20 (twenty) months old in my subconscious.

Now you say how did this happen what was the cause and this I can assure you it does happen to many.

As a 20 month old child coming down the stairway from the upstairs bedroom on a Christmas morning saw a Green Spruce tree with all the decorations on it. WOW I'm going to go and explore and see what this is all about and as I make my way close to the tree I hear a very loud command NO. That just froze me in my tracks, my older sister seeing me and afraid for me getting hurt just shouted out NO. That very suggestion of NO was so powerful like a hypnotic suggestion and that went right into my subconscious mind as a programming statement. The internal decision that was made then was "I can't do what I want".

That particular aspect within me its function was to not let me succeed, why because I had installed in me a belief that I could not do what I wanted.

That is the power of a decision (a belief) which is an Aspect, and it can & does affect the rest of your life. Unless, unless you can find a way to go back in and re-view, re-decide again.

<u>Now here's a question</u>, -- How many decision have you made (in the past) that could be directly affecting your life right now? Good ok, Bad – it's time to re-decide again.

Now who would of thought that good intentions of another because of fear of me maybe getting hurt, would have such an effect on my life for the next 45 or so years. As a child, me, 20 months old, of just making an internal <u>"unconscious"</u> decision thinking that I can't do what I want would have such an impact on one's life. And all I wanted to do at that time was to go and touch a tree, because it wasn't there the night before.

This has been one of the greatest lessons of my life on how we as human beings got so brainwashed / conditioned into thinking what we now think.

Because of the work that I now do, I'll share one story from a client that I was working with.

A man in his early 20's came to see me, because he had heard of the work that I was doing, he was very stressed out and lots of anxiety. So we talked for a bit to exchange information asked him what he wanted and how this process would develop. This was his third "intimate" relationship with another beautiful women and because of the intimacy he was starting to panic. He was saying that every time things get intimate something comes over him and he has to break it apart. So with that we were able to go inside and converse with this aspect (this is a special process developed) and find out the original cause, original decision that was made to cause this panic this anxiety. To cut the story shot and get to the point at seven months while still in his mother's womb made a decision that it really hurts to be intimate with someone. <u>Did</u> you get that, or read that, a DECISION made in the womb at 7 months, can have an effect on your life some 20 yrs. later!

The reason being was that the husband an alcoholic would come home from work, mostly always drunk and would beat up on his wife. The child being in the womb would get bounced around, maybe hit and could feel the hurt and so on.

Once the internal self knew and the aspect who's function was to protect knew that, that was then and this is now, no longer needed to protect, because protection was not needed. All the energy that was associated with this was also changed and given a different function, one of love.

Another example: A young girl at six years old working with her mother cooking in the kitchen. Her mother was very tiny / small in body and her health was never very good. This one day in her perception seeing her mother in poor health, decided that to be small and tiny is to be sick. So in her subconscious mind was created an Aspect to put on weight because of not wanting to be sick. Much later in life 25 years or so she kept trying to lose weight. She tried every diet possible, nothing seemed to work or was working for her.

Then one day she went through this process of "reverse engineering" finding the original cause, that I do and lord and be hold she rediscovered that decision she did at six. In negotiating with that aspect in the subconscious mind, it was able to let all that go, including the energy that supported it, change the thought about being sick and associated with weight. She was able to lose weight without changing her way of eating. Of course to eat in moderation is also good.

Now one thing to know and become aware of here is that everything in memory (the subconscious mind) "is DATED". <u>Every choice that was decided on is dated.</u> Ask inside to the part of you that does this function if it will communicate with you in consciousness, (as if you're taking to another person inside of you) and when it does, explore it all. ***<u>By the way there Is a very special process that is best followed when doing this kind of work.</u>***

We've discovered with this work that one can bring things in from the past, as in past lives, and I'm told even up to seven generation back and more. Aspects of our fore fathers and here were trying to live normal lives. To succeed in life to what were told and to believe that's the way it is. "Hog wash" been there done that.

Now another thing about aspects or parts (as I like to call them), is that you can be in an others energy field and you can pick them up thinking that there yours. Now that there in your energy field they feed off your energy. It's like a parasite.

CHAPTER

7

Parasites

Parasites are also aspects / viruses that have a reality of their own. They came into your system, either by decision of or you bought a belief from someone or just being in someone else's energy field. Now these parasites feed off your energy field, maybe they were part of the dense mass consciousness thoughts in the either's.

These parasites you may not even know that they are, because you may think / believe that it's normal to feel this way, yet it isn't it's not you. But (there's this but again) if you are in agreement with it and it will persuade you to be in agreement with it, then you have lost and it wins again keeping you enslaved.

With some training and understanding now, once you know that you're God and you go right to the core of your being, from that core of your being, you can overcome any parasite(s), any aspect.

A great book to read here, (it's written as a Science fiction) but truly discovered knowledge, is "MIND PARASITES" Author? Slips me at the moment. He had discovered his own inner spark of creation.

- Imagination -- a great tool

The Imagination is one of the most powerful tools we have, because without it, we'd still be in the dark. Our imagination is connected to our hearts and our hearts our connected to our Soul.

One of the big problems in humanity right now is depression, many are suffering from depression and it's rampant throughout the world. The drugs to try to solve this is amazing, the reason being is that people have shut down their own creativity. And creativity is connected to the Imagination.

Have you ever heard people say, "Oh, it's only your Imagination"! What are they saying? Many have a belief that the imagination isn't real – Yet it's real it's just another dimension, the dimension of thought which is the 4th. Dimension. The 4th. and 3rd. dimensions work in pairs, first is thought then as one works with the energy, the vibrations slow down and now it's more dense and now in the 3rd. in matter.

There's a very good reason for this lapse time between the fourth and the third dimension and that is so you can still change your mind before it materializes in matter.

The reason people have shut down their creative abilities, their creative talents, is because they are not using their imagination, remember for many the imagination isn't real. Yet that's where everything starts, it all starts with our imagination. This book that you're holding and reading started as a thought, in the imagination and now you're touching and reading it, is it real?

Imagine for a moment, as an example, Mom is at the kitchen table and she's wondering what to do and have for supper. A picture comes to her mind of a big double decker chocolate cake. And she thinks hum, the family would love that for a dessert. So she gets up and goes to the cupboard and starts to pull out all the ingrediences needed. First the bowls, spoons etc… flour, eggs, vanilla, water, etc… Once it's all mixed she puts it in a pan and sticks it in the oven.

Then guess what? After you've finished the meal, out comes a big double decker chocolate cake and it's delicious, can even have ice cream with it.

The thing is where did it start? It started in the mind, in the imagination. It started with a thought and she said yes, that's what I want to create and have for supper for the family and she did.

Many have lost hope in their lives, they have shut down their hopes and dreams, because of certain traumas, trapped emotions that they've experienced as a child.

I was very fortunate in my life to start a career in creating and building new kitchen cabinets for people. I always had to use my imagination and picture the cupboards in my mind first, put them down on paper, so the client could see what the finished product would look like. Lots of times I would work with them so they could have some say so on the creation of their kitchen. The result was many happy customers.

If you are not using your imagination, you're not allowing your spirit to be part of your life. Spirit is very creative, you are a creator, you've just allowed others to cripple your imagination by saying it isn't real. It's time to change that belief in your subconscious mind so that it can start working for you instead of against you.

Basically this is what this book is all about, how you can go back into your subconscious mind find the old belief, delete it and install a new belief that now your subconscious will take and work with. (see the section on aspects pg. 30 & 53), (and on decisions pg. 42.)

We all have an image of self, called your self-image. In many religions they say that we were made in his image, Gods image. But many of us have developed an image inside of ourselves, in our subconscious mind, because of what we told our-selves and what others told us of what we are. So then we create our world according to our image, our beliefs of what we are inside. When you use your Imagination you are putting your image in motion and the law of attraction works every time.

This tool one of the most powerful tools I'm told is our imagination. So here at this point one can meditate and imagine what this would look like. Say this thing is in your landscape, in your envoirment, whatever ugly thing this would be.

Picture it & feel the energy of it, then take from the store room cabinet in your Imagination or anything like that a LASER gun and just blast it to simdariens making sure that all the energy is gone. If you have to give it another blast do it, just to make sure the energy is all disappeared. One does not want any residue around, and you can also get a vacuum cleaner and suck it all up so that everything is clean.

Then what you do after that is fill it back up with good clean pure GOLDEN energy and maybe a thought of "I love me", and beautiful golden sparks of pure energy keep filling up the space / landscape up in to all those empty spaces that were emptied.

One does prana breathing, prana particles, maybe see them as water drops or snow flakes, that are in the air, just breath them in and fill all those places inside of self that were emptied. There's no right way or wrong way to do this.

Relationships & the Mind

We live in a binary system and with our conscious mind "Judge" (we learn to judge) about what's right and about what's wrong, and from there make something real, we say it's real but it's really just an illusion, everything is illusion, hypnotic suggestion by others. And then there are overlays upon overlays that are built upon each other, their actually lies. So if reality (what we think is reality) is built on lies and hypnotic suggestions from anything outside of you, guess how come we as a society are such a mess. *Typically, hypnotic overlays and belief systems are interjected from outside sources such as parents, teachers, churches, governments, businesses and society. These overlays are "unconsciously" accepted into a person's mind & belief structure and soon manifest in their everyday lives.*

Our subconscious sees both sides of everything it experiences things as a whole, but because of our personality and perception of circumstances and the decisions one makes the subconscious "may" only show us one side of the coin. It sees

/ knows both sides, problem / solution. One side is problem the other is solution. If a person would not separate the 2, as in duality or polarity then it's just an event. Neither good nor bad just an event, you may like it and you may not, that's then just a preference.

Because we live in a binary world both polarities are present all the time, and we use this world of abstract to learn from or else how would one learn and from there make choices. This I like this I don't, but again where do my choices come from mostly from prier decisions which are in our memory files. The biggest problem is what are these memories based on, others suggestions and lies and in all of that what is true?

Example say:

A child growing up with their parents sometimes sees that the parents are arguing about something, could be anything. Say the father is self-centered; arrogant puts his wife down all the time. The child sees all of that and makes a judgment / decision about what's happening. Now the decision one makes on a circumstance such as this can vary quite a bit. Say it's a daughter (could be a son) and she (he) quietly thinks I would not take that, I would leave I would not stay in such a situation. Now remember the subconscious sees both the problem and solution, but in this situation the child is not in a position of authority or power that could apply the solution.

Now here's the *sticker* and please follow this through. We are all here to learn and it doesn't matter what we learn, just that we learn. Remember I said that the subconscious sees holistically, (as a whole), so what the mind will then do, later on in life, set up a situation to apply the solution. Say it's a lady (could be a man, this applies to both sexes), will get in a relationship with a man so she can apply the solution. She will leave the man (husband), and the subconscious will say "there problem solved", *what she was actually doing is solving her parents relationship in her own relationship.*

Once a person realizes that, that you're trying to solve your parent's relationship in your own, you don't have to create the problem in order to solve it. It had nothing to do with you in the first place; it was just your perception of a situation. All these choices that one's made in the past, because of many perceptions and hypnotic suggestions and lies and overlays upon overlays. Many people's relationships and break ups are because of perceptions / choices and decisions and it had nothing to do with them personally.

Now here is how this is done or "asked of the other" when you would want to help in relationship.

Ask the other person this question (and play with this –Pretend). If you were your mother, in other words put you're self in your mothers shoes, and if you were her. What would you have done differently? Now the first thing that comes up, "first response" is usually the right answer. Now see how this would apply to your life situation, if it does realize that you don't have to solve your parent's relationship in your own. If not or there's no perceived problem then forget it, it does not apply to you then. If you're a man then put yourself in your father's shoes and ask the same question. What would you have done differently and see how that applies to your situation.

According to the spirits (from the other side of the veil) that I worked with, this is one of the most important questions in the world, "there are 10 most important questions they say" this was the first one.

CHAPTER

8

Number 2 question is money

Another perceived problem in humanity is money – What we've been told about money and what it is. Really money is an exchange, it simplified everything, and it's convenient. Money is also related to values, values of this and value of that. Again we could be talking of / about the same thing but there's a different value put upon it. Now nearly, everything is overvalued and some things undervalued.

There are people, a certain mind set, that pay any price for what they want it's not too much of a concern. Another mind set, say that's way too much, I just won't pay that and then do without. Right now society is going through a restructuring of this entire system, what we call money. This started with a thought and the thought is "we can't keep going this way". A conclusion was drawn on the movement that society / humanity could not continue this way and that started the de-structuring of money.

One of the general things that money gives you is "time", time to choose, time to decide and convenience. You don't have to decide now, you don't have to buy now, you can later, and it's more of a conscious decision and not an unconscious decision, one is not coming from a position of lack. The saying that it takes less time to make the second million then the first million is that one takes more risks.

Brain lock and hypnosis

At this time (2010) about 87% of the population is under a hypnotic trans-state and don't even know it. They (humanity) are in a hypnotic state designed by the matrix, and energy that knows how to control energy & have every one follow, so everyone is in a brain lock and go along with that as sheep. It's an energy (a way of thinking) that gets you to focus outside of yourself, focus outside anything other than yourself; because you were born in sin they say. You were born in the physical which is of the none-spiritual so you must be bad, and you are here now as a punishment and not as a celebration of life.

The biggest problem humanity has now is to de-condition themselves, to un-brainwash themselves and to rediscover their own inner truth, what's true for them.

To stay neutral is probably the best thing to do, a Master will not necessarily say yea or nay, because he or she knows that everything will change. One of the best things to do is to not judge anything, "not judge anything" including yourself. Because by judging this is good this is bad etc… sets up duality / polarity, which create the illusion & density of the 3rd. dimension. Yes we are here in this contras "3'D" because we learn in / from the contras as to direction and to experience from, because we are here to experience the experience of experiencing and that's how one evolves.

So to not judge the self as well, which is probably very difficult for many because of how we have all been conditioned / brainwashed into thinking and believing what is real. Every one of us has developed filters of perception and don't always see the same thing the same way, even though we are looking at the same thing. One person is using rose colored glasses and the other green or yellow colored glasses. So every one of us distorts reality by our colored glasses & filters, which are beliefs and values, again learn from others say so.

People get stuck in that illusion and keep re-creating it over and over again. One projects from the memories of the past onto the future and re-creating their past over and over again and they keep getting the same results. So if one sees lack in their world then one will create lack, if one has no self-value, self-worth then one will reap things of unworthiness.

Each and every person is a self-fulfilling Prophecy of their own perception. So if one could / would stop judging themselves & others and see everything as perfect, Perfect just the way it is – without adding (from one self) onto reality a pre-prescribed value or belief one stays neutral and can consciously choose a preference of what they want instead. That's Mastery, so one could be in the world but not of it.

3D (the 3rd. dimension) is very seductive; it draws one into the energy of the physical. It's like the sexual energy, very powerful, very seductive, one can be drawn into it sometimes without realizing that one was drawn into it. It would be like Sam & Delilah, she was so beautiful and with her sexual energy right up front it was very difficult for Samson to refuse her suppose it love.

It would be just like some beautiful women in my life right now, that if they came onto me, what would I choose? It really depends on how conscious I am and in the now & what would I want to experience. Being single is easier to choose one would not have to add anything from the past onto the event, except joy and perfection. Lots of people though would add <u>GUILT</u> because thoughts and beliefs of the past. Guilt prevents enjoyment, living life fully.

Guilt Prevents Enjoyment

Where does guilt come from? Where did you learn what guilt is? It's usually to do with beliefs and values, where / when were these established and are they still applicable? What if a person was to transform / revise ones beliefs to current times? Guilt prevents enjoyment. Guilt keeps us separate from our own spirit. Guilt is negativity projected backwards and it will rob you of your energies. There is so much energy right now that is being suppressed because of our beliefs and values, which does not allow room for any creativity and growth. Yes one can justify anything one wants to get our needs met, but now with this new energy one also needs to take responsibility for every action one takes.

The more responsibility one takes, the more energy one can attract / receive. If one does choose, to create now with love, with the energy of love onto it, that will return a thousand fold, it's the same law. What one puts out is what one gets in return. Just to add here, another perspective, am I creating consciously or is it an aspect of me, within me that has surfaced into my conscious and adding its own views from its self on to my reality. What would be the result of this?

See all energies want to continue to survive, the good, the bad, the ugly. These are all within one self, which is why it's become really important to master ones thoughts. Which one would you allow to create your world, your reality? None of this is really new were just becoming "more conscious" of how all this energy works.

We're all just becoming more aware of ourselves and everything else. We're all going through a shift, a planetary shift, and its call the GREAT SHIFT IN CONSCIOUSNESS. This window of opportunity, (a 25yr. window) started in 1987, the harmonic convergence and will go till December 21st. 2012. That's why there's a big thing right now about 2012, The End Times. This energy movement really started back in the early nineteen hundreds.

Causes of Separation and Division

The causes of separation and division to others and then to self. The initial steps in separation and division starts as a child, mostly because of what were told by our parents and others close by. Their fears / values / beliefs are projected onto the child as a truth, as a reality. Therefore the child (innocent as can be and a sponge for knowledge) is being conditioned by such thoughts / rules / values and takes it on as a truth and reality.

An old Chinese proverb; do not pass your beliefs and values onto your children, for they were born of a different time.

I always wanted to touch and feel, *"is a natural"* process of human nature. To want to touch and feel is a natural process of how a child learns, so to touch and feel is how knowledge is attained in one's life. In touching and feeling is also what develops the personality.

So let's say that as a child one is curious on how things work, say as in playing being a doctor. You be the doctor or I be the doctor and one starts to examine, there's curiosity, this and that, their curious and on and on. Then children (say) start exploring their sexual areas and that's when people come in and say, well not in those areas. That's a no, no. That's the first step in creating separation / divisions and the learning stops.

This creates a separation between self and others and every times one separates self from other, creates a division between self and self. This leads to more separation & more separation until one gets to the point of questioning "Who am I". One has lost touch with one's body and most of the time people are not even in their bodies any more. People are not grounded, not here, Oh there is a body but nobody is home. Knock, Knock who's there? Mostly everyone has been conditioned to think this way, move up into your head, don't feel "THINK" and this gets everyone to go mental, into their heads.

Then the mental and the body become separate, for many people now there's no connection to the body. The body has just about become foreign – that's when disease sets in, to try to get us back into what we are. We are, are bodies and much more – we are much more than our bodies, we are Spirit beings having a human experience. The body is an extension of one's spirit, and uses the body as an extension of its self to learn and grow / evolve. That's why it's good and healthy to touch and feel and to enjoy one's body, to enjoy life, the spirit of being.

To enjoy life is to enjoy creating and to know that one is source. I am the source of my being the source of my creation. Therefore "I am" – "I am that I am" a soiverient being.

Follow Your Heart

Follow your heart and ask your mind to understand what your heart is saying. Then you have a true relationship with your higher self. Once the mind lets go control and starts to / begins to serve the body / soul, the authentic self can experience some of the greatest lessons and with joy.

Most people when they start on their spiritual path and development look outside of themselves, for others truths, which is good not bad. After while though a person needs to look inside and discover their own truths. The big problem thought with looking in side, is that people don't like themselves, there's nothing inside that's any good, so one looks out side. What are your truths and where did you learn them from, what are the results / extensions of those truths? What is the byproduct of them? What kind of reality do they create? Do those truths unite everyone or separate? Yes it's good to learn from others, from each other, but what's your truth, what do you choose? If you find out later something different you can always change it, that's your god given right. Then you become the cause and not at the effect of. At the effect of someone else's cause, that's their truth. People have forgotten the heart, the heart were everything resides. In matters of the heart the heart matters.

Become self-realized as one and the same, that's what is the Alpha and the Omega, the one & the only. The marriage of both polarities, the neutral zone or all of the terminologies that you have heard. Once you recognize this ability, this truth, then all of the other sciences, plus projections, possibilities – all of these then will become simply the next truth. It will simply be how things are.

When you finally see yourself with all the knowledge you've accumulated – the result is I'am, -- I'am that I'am. You are what you are and the complete acceptance of what you are is what makes the difference. Once you completely accept what you are, you are ready to enjoy life. There's no more judgment, no more guilt, no more shame, no more remorse. Bless it be – I'am.

CHAPTER

9

It's cellular

The science of healing all the cells in the body. Every cell has memory of its creator, and its purpose for being. Yet the DNA is controlled by signals from outside the cell, including the energetic messages emanating from our positive and negative thoughts. In other words, cells respond to energy, to thoughts, to imaginings.

According to Scientist "Bruce Lipton", a biologist, in his book "the biology of belief" writes that each cell has 3 membranes that nutrient passes through for its food and also to discard the waste (toxins) back out. He's also discovered that these membranes can get contaminated, become ridged, because of the foods that we eat and then don't allow the toxins to be released. He describes these membranes as a slice of bread, which is quite porous and when one would pour water on it, gradually the water would come through the other side, then the next membrane, and the next membrane to the core of the cell. Then in return the wastes / toxins would be released the same way in reverse.

What happens because of what we eat, and our way of life, to busy a schedule, stress these membranes get plugged so all the toxins can't get out, the cell starts to slow down, because it's not being nourished properly, becomes a dis-eased cell (unbalanced cell). The way out of this is to change our way of living, our food intake, exercises and mostly change our way of thinking about ourselves and the world.

Another way (and I know people will shrug at this) is to communicate with the cell itself and to find out what its views are, it's perception of reality is. It has one you know and to find out when all of this started and what needs to be done so that it (the cell) can become healthy again and function like a normal cell.

The Higher Self --------- 2013
Now is the time to Connect

Now is the time to present the Self to your own personality, your beingness, but one must understand what the self is; for the self is a very great being.

The Self is a very great truth. The Self is your beingness – what is presently here, your body is simply an aspect of Self. The Self contains your body, the Self contains your ideas and the Self relates to the soul more whole, then any other part of your being.

The Self understands, it knows, it feels, but it exists beyond your mental body it exists beyond your Emotional body, it exists beyond the mind. The Self is the agent of the soul.

The Self is; -- The Self is the individual being that you are. It's a collective aspect of truth. It is an unfoldment, it is an awareness. The Self is the advanced aspect, the self in essence is a Sentience. The Self expands weather or not your life does. Your Self becomes more present weather or not your personality makes any progress what's so ever. The Self becomes more worldly, more galactic, more universal. The Self collects your true memories, not what your mind recalls. So the Self is the gift that you are. The Self does not judge, the Self is incapable of it.

In order not to judge, one simply offers the Self, the expanded Self as the reference point. And then it is not possible for judgement to enter, because the Self exist beyond it.

This is the time then of the Self and it is the Self that can create for you, all of the envoirment much better than your personality can or your common direction can and such.

Your personality knows truth, your Self knows greater truths, and it is the Self that will move forward into the 5th. dimension. Yes the Self will carry the personality with it, but it will be an adjusted personality, just a bit different then it is now. An adjusted personality is one that is more linked to the Self. A personality that does not necessarily look forward and backwards, into all sides before making a decision. Linked with the Self, the stride is more assured.

Will all human beings make such a stride, in the future yes, but in their own way. Just as now, there are those that grow very quickly and there are those that do not. The expanded Self will be the same.

The Self then has a greater presence then and directs life. It directs one to build, to create ones envoirment, in which the personality will all so dwell. The 5th. dimensional envoirment will be created for the Self and what the Self creates. Divine proportion is how you allow the Self to be more than the present moment. Divine proportion is based upon theory of geometry and for the most part these are understood but not completely so. All that is understood now of geometry is of the 3rd. dimension.

The Self understands how to take that theory and now apply it through time into and through dimensions. This makes it present, this makes it available to the Self and to the Soul and to the past and to the present and into the future. So time begins to shift now, shifts your reality and the shifting time, is the shifting sands. It will convert all, it will convert currencies, it will convert thoughts, it will convert feelings, it will expand ideas, and creativity will once again return.

To understand the Self and to understand the person and to understand ones envoirment is to be creative. And this you are invited to do now.

Time and place and dimensions are an awareness. Time and place and dimensions create Ideas, and all of these subjects reveal themselves to you now. Your awareness now will bring all of this to you. A creative idea, a true creative idea, is one that can manifest in a very short amount of time. The longer an idea takes to be made manifest, the more flawed it is.

Time & the speed of light are one, and the speed of light is now changing. The faster your mind works, the more your thoughts will slow and the more you will appear to your thoughts. Now you can barely control your thoughts. Into and through, into and through, into and through. Most of your thoughts are really not your own (95%), they belong to others. They belong to the past, they hang around the atoms of the air because they have not been dismissed. And so many things are made manifest now, simply because there is an accumulation of energy associated with the subject.

The wars – the planets wars, in the middle east is such one example. Because the thoughts did not die down. Because they were transferred from mind to mind, from office to office, from government to government, they expanded the idea and they became manifest. If it was simply an idea and the mind said instead Peace, let there be peace all of the other thoughts would have fallen away.

And it is the same now. "WHAT EVER YOU FEED WILL CONTINUE TO GROW". What you focus on is usually what will manifest. We may use the word terrorism for instance, how often is it used? How often is it said? How often is it thought and it continues to make it a reality. It is one of the things that's keeping humanity in density and the 3rd. dimension.

How often do the same thoughts about yourself, come through your mind? If you buy them they are yours. Why would you buy anything that is less than the greatness that you are?

On Cancer

How Cancer cells are formed

Cancer starts with a thought, a thought of low frequency, low energy. New cells are being created in the body all the time and it depends on the state and envoirment one is in. As cells go through the blood stream it tries to find another onto it's-self. Gradually other cells of low energy, of similar frequency find each other, they start to form like a gang does. And they go about stealing energy from other cells to survive. They become a burden to the body. The rest of the body would wish that they would just go away but they have become more dense, more solid.

All of the dense thoughts, they gather together, breathe as one, move through the system disrupting the whole. The medical team calls these cancer cells, radical cells or free radicals. These cells / thoughts will not pass through the 1212 gateway, the 5th. dimensional gateway they are to solid, to dense, to ill and they will destroy themselves or move into the back ground.

All of your thoughts that are to heavy, to dense, must be brought up to the surface, so they can be "Transformed". *__And this can be done through a very special process__*, "**called reverse engineering**". It's to take a dis-eased cell back to before it went out of balance, and then to bring it forward but now on a different path, now it's at ease in other words balanced.

But people usually don't do this, until it's too late. Then they go through the old system hoping that they can be healed but it usually doesn't work, a greater percentage leave the planet and have to come back and try again.

So many people right now are very uncomfortable with the exterior envoirment. It's chaos and tough out there, so there looking inside to create an inner envoirment, thinking that that would be enough. In a short period of time they will find out that, that was not enough.

Most of the thoughts are heavy and dense from mass consciousness (95%), one needs to learn how to bring to the surface and review, see differently and clear and cleanse the energy that supported those thoughts. Maybe one will have to detach from the familiar and let go.

True Change

Imagine a boat, a big boat, a cruise line with 12 / 13 floors, with many rooms on each floor, swimming pool top upper deck, saunas and the like. Now this is your body, your vessel, this is your life. When we first come into the body, into this ship, one does not have the way with all it takes years. That's why a child needs parents or someone to assist, support in one's growth. Now this ship needs a captain, a captain that set's the direction and the purpose of a journey.

So the first few years it goes through a school, a school of learning about itself (the captain) and about the ship (the body). The parents are its prime source of input and brothers & sisters if any, uncles & aunts, neighbors, schools etc... From this entire exterior world it learns about life, or so it would seem. From this makes decisions and choices establishes values / rules, about its self and reality, so it thinks.

At first one does not have the way with all, so it gives authority over to the subconscious mind the task / job of making sure it survives. The prime function of the subconscious is survival, survival of the body and its functions and survival of the personality that the self is developing. Now there's basically only two fears a person is born with fear of falling and fear of loud noises, survival based, all other fears are learnt.

Please always keep in mind this boat / ship and all the different rooms, floors in & on it to get to understand the reality & complexities of this. Every time a person (the personality) that resides in that body, makes a decision about life & or self is like hiring an employee on the ship to carry on the task of that decision. That employee then has a room in that ship to carry out that function, that task. Every time it is triggered it comes into consciousness and does that function, after while it just becomes automatic one does not have to think.

Say at first for example, to tie your shoes, one needs to focus on what one is doing, tying your shoes then over time it gets easier and easier until it becomes automatic. One can then even think of something else altogether and still tie ones shoes. Everything follows this process, learning to cook, to sew, to drive a vehicle, to play music etc… At first to put ones attention and focus on to a task and with some "trial and error" learns how to do many things, then they all become automatic.

<u>This is also what creates many problems later on in life, let me explain.</u> How many decisions does one make in the first few years in one's life? Hundreds, thousands of decisions are made, so now you have thousands of employees ***"that are hired by you"*** to carry out these different functions. Each employee may / will develop a

sub-personality of its own, within the vessel (the body, subconscious mind).

These employees, for sake of understanding where were going with all of this; we will call them ***Parts or Aspects.*** Different parts of self, different aspects of self. These aspects / parts can and do develop a perception of reality on their own.

They develop a sub-personality of their own, that operates within the body and come into consciousness when activated or when their triggered to come into consciousness. Because that was their function their purpose for being, that's what they were hired for. These aspects / parts develop their own sense of time / space & reality and the only way that they know what's going on is what you tell them. Because they're in their room you see with no windows. They may not even know or even be aware of other aspects / parts that are in other rooms & on different floors.

They may have had the opportunity to every now and then to meet & interact with other aspects / parts, depending the different functions / jobs they all have. Some of them have no Idea and concept of time, they have no idea that time has even gone by. They may not know that a week has gone by, that a month, a year / year(s) has gone by. Because they're in this room with no windows and no one has informed them, interacted with them so there's no notice of time. Some time as a whole one may not even know that they exist anymore, they've been forgotten. Yet they keep doing the same job over and over again, that's what they were hired to do.

You the personality may of aged in physical years to 30-40-50-60- yrs. yet some parts / aspects are still only 3, 4, 5, 6 yrs. old inside the self, they have not aged. They did not perceive time go by.

People tend to live in the past, they look at memory, which is on file, for direction and then project that thought into the future, so in a sense they are living their past.

See there is no past and there is no future there is only now, but what humanity does, because of being stuck in 3D, 3rd. dimension, a polarized world with time, see it as past present & future.

Do you have issues in your life that have been around for a long time? If one keeps applying the same solution to a different problem, you'll continue getting the same results, over and over again. ***MORE OF THE SAME IS NOT THE ANSWER.***

And if you keep living other people's truths, you'll get their results, not yours. What are your truths? And what do you want? Are you the captain of your ship / vessel / life, or did you give over the command of your life to an aspect, to run it for you?

This is what many people have done, given up command to the subconscious and now the subconscious is telling them what it is, and the personality goes along with it. This is what many people have done right now at least 80 to 85 % of the population in the world is unconscious. They (you) are not conscious; you may think that you are, but that is only an aspect letting you think that you are.

__ Are you being what you want to be?

__ Are you doing what you want to do?

__ Do you have in your life what you want?

If yes, then I'd say you're the captain of your life.

If not then it's more than likely you are allowing different aspects (parts) to run your life. Aspects live in the past, from memory, a memory on file in your subconscious / unconscious. So aspects live in the past, you're looking in the rear view mirror (say of your car) and seeing your future, which is your past. So if you can find a way from / in this book to heal your past, then your future will be different. Your future will be your past healed.

An other way of saying it, is people are walking back-wards in time. Walking backwards in time means, you're looking back at your memories to know what to choose for your future. So really you're re-creating your past.

This may seem like a play on words, yet if you understand what's being said here, you can have a great future. Learning to reset / restructure / re-engineer your past is one of the main *"KEYS"* to a great future.

The KEY(S) then is in being able to gain access to all PARTS / ASPECTS of, in the Subconscious and to re-structure / called "reverse engineer" of old Ideas, beliefs, values, rules to all new possibilities, potentials. Change your contract, vaporize your anxieties, and clear all old emotional baggage.

Raise your vibrations by falling in love with yourself.

It's time to write yourself a new script. What part do you want to play? We suggest that you become the main actor of this new script, and not just a fill in, with small parts to play.

Learn to play well together.